TABLE OF CONTENTS

CHAPTER 1

DEFINING VIOLENCE

Images of **violence** are everywhere in the media you consume. You can see them in the news. You can see them at the movies. You can see them in video games. Depictions of strength and brutality are common in music, movies, and books. They're also found in social media, sports, and even in clothing.

Violence is aggression that has as its goal extreme physical harm, such as injury or even death. Aggression is any behavior intended to harm another person. The harm can be psychological or physical.

It's important to know where today's trends come from in order to understand what kind of influence they have on your life. Many of society's values and beliefs are reflected in the messages we see and hear in the media. But our values also can be influenced by those same messages.

Violence is everywhere in popular culture these days, from movies and music to video games and sports.

Video games contain some of the most violent content that children and teenagers encounter in the media.

To better understand how common violence has become in today's society, look for it in each area of popular culture. Ask yourself a few questions about what you're seeing:

- Who creates violent messages and why?
- What tools are used to get your attention?

- How might someone who is different from you interpret the message?
- Consider what's missing from the picture. Does that change how you view it?

Questioning what you see can help you understand why violence is such a controversial topic.

JUST A GAME?

Video games have been widely popular since the 1970s. They've also been controversial, pretty much from the start. Graphics have become more lifelike. The violence in the games seems more realistic. Does playing a violent video game make you a more aggressive person?

In most of these games, players are not just watching the violence happen on the screen. They are directing characters to commit those violent acts. Also, acts of violence are often rewarded in video games. Instead of going to prison for killing another player, you might be rewarded by advancing to the next level. That could affect how a child understands the consequences of violence in real life.

CHAPTER 2

REAL VS. VIRTUAL VIOLENCE

The media can influence how people behave in public and in their homes. But you have to see or hear that media before it can influence your decisions. How does the media try to get your attention?

Young people once looked mostly to their friends, family members, and teachers for guidance. They watched those close to them make decisions, both good and bad. Then they learned from observing the consequences of those decisions.

Today, many people also base their values on what is popular, especially with celebrities. Your favorite musician, film director, or author can have a strong influence on your own beliefs. A musician might record a song about a violent relationship, like the one between singers Rihanna and Chris Brown. Rihanna appeared to address that violence in the song "Love the Way You Lie." Her vocals include this passage:

The lyrics to "Love the Way You Lie" seem to address Rihanna's violent relationship with Chris Brown.

Just gonna stand there and watch me burn

But that's alright because I like the way it hurts

Most of her fans likely know that Rihanna stayed with Brown after he abused her. Those lyrics

Tom and Jerry were a cartoon cat and mouse whose violent antics were depicted as humorous, not scary.

might lead them to support the decision to remain in an abusive relationship.

But violence in pop culture isn't always that literal. Cartoons often include examples of violence played for comic effect. When Homer strangles Bart for acting up in *The Simpsons*, the abuse looks **humorous** rather than dangerous or scary.

Children tend to copy, or **mimic**, what they see and hear in their everyday lives. So if children watch television shows that contain "humorous" violence, they might be more likely to commit aggressive acts. That's because it looked fun, not harmful, on TV.

It can be difficult for children to understand the difference between fictional and real violence. Children who define violence based only on what they have seen on-screen could be less likely to view it seriously if it

THE VIOLENT HISTORY OF CARTOONS

SpongeBob SquarePants has been on the air since 1999. It is the most watched television show on Nickelodeon. Although many people enjoy this cartoon, its displays of violence are almost too **subtle** to notice their effect. A character getting run over by a steamroller is played as a joke. *SpongeBob* is definitely not the first cartoon to do this. In 1940, the cartoon *Tom and Jerry* debuted. It featured a mouse who continuously outsmarted the cat, often using violence in a humorous way. In *The Simpsons*, the children cackle at the brutal antics of a similar cat and mouse named Itchy and Scratchy. The creators of *The Simpsons* use Itchy and Scratchy to show how outrageous televised violence aimed at children has become. Cartoons that contain exaggerated violence have been around for decades. One study showed that about 90 percent of pediatricians believe that violent media can increase aggression in children.

Children who watch too much violence on TV can become desensitized to its effects in real life.

happens in real life. This is called **desensitizing**. After seeing so much violence in the media, people can become numb to the pain and suffering of those in the real world.

Research has shown that some children who are exposed to violence in the media show early signs of aggressive behavior. They also can demonstrate a lack of **empathy** for the victims of violence. And they are often desensitized to other violence they witness.

[21ST CENTURY SKILLS LIBRARY]

When the media uses **persuasion**, it tries to convince its audience to accept certain ideas. **Repetition** is a technique used to persuade an audience that violence is acceptable. Violent acts can seem normal if they are repeated often enough in the media.

The violence in cartoons such as *SpongeBob SquarePants* is different from the violence in shows aimed at adults, such as *American Horror Story*. But the type of violence is not important. What matters is that violence can be found on almost every TV channel. That repetition can make it seem more acceptable.

SUPERHERO VIOLENCE

Many movies, video games, and even toys that are made for children have a connection to pop-culture violence. The superheroes in Marvel's *The Avengers* seem to be everywhere: movies, TV, toys, books, and video games. You can find their images on T-shirts and school supplies. Although these superheroes specialize in destroying their enemies, they still represent a type of violence. Research has shown that superheroes model aggressive behavior that boys are more likely to mimic.

CHAPTER 3

VIEWPOINTS CAN VARY

If you examine violence in today's pop culture, you will see how often it appears. But does everyone view violence in the same way? How a person responds to violence depends on a variety of factors.

What you see or hear on the surface of any message is called the **text**. Everyone who sees or hears a message is exposed to the same text. But the way a person feels about it is different for each individual. That's because of the **subtext** of a message. The subtext is not necessarily seen or heard by everyone. Rather, people have their own ideas about the message. We respond differently to song lyrics, a mixed martial arts match, or a scene from a violent movie. Your interpretation of the subtext stems from your morals, values, and opinions. Those are often based on experiences and knowledge gained during childhood and your early teenage years.

Some people are entertained by mixed martial arts combat. Others see it as needlessly violent.

Sometimes, however, the public's reaction is almost **unanimous**. Most people had a strong negative reaction when the retail store Urban Outfitters released its "Vintage Kent State Sweatshirt." It appeared to be bloodstained and frayed as though it had been riddled with bullets. Many thought that it was a cruel reference

Kent State students help a fallen friend after National Guard troops opened fire on a crowd of protestors in 1970.

PUMPED UP KICKS

In 2010, the song "Pumped Up Kicks" was a big hit for a group called Foster the People. The song had a danceable beat and a sing-along chorus. But its lyrics were less than pleasant. The song tells the story of a child preparing to bring a gun to school.

All the other kids with the pumped up kicks
You better run, better run, outrun my gun ...
You better run, better run, faster than my bullet

When the song was played on radio stations across the country, it seemed as if the lyrics went unnoticed. Perhaps the catchy beat and cheerful voices threw listeners off track. Those who didn't notice the violent lyrics might have been desensitized to that type of message. But research has shown that violent lyrics can increase aggressive thoughts and feelings even if people don't notice the lyrics.

to the infamous 1970 shooting at Kent State University in which four students were killed.

Urban Outfitters said that it had not meant to make the sweatshirt appear bloodstained. Although the actual sweatshirt *looked* the same to each individual, people had different views of the underlying message. Some of

Many Americans turned against the Vietnam War effort after seeing televised footage of violence from the battlefield.

them remembered that tragic day or had witnessed other school shootings. They likely had a negative view of the sweatshirt, based on their experiences. But others had not experienced similar violence. Or they had become desensitized to it through its repetition in pop culture. They probably thought the backlash was an overreaction.

In response to the outcry, Urban Outfitters removed the sweatshirt from its website. It has never been sold in stores.

CHAPTER 4

WHAT MEDIA LEAVES OUT

Walk down the magazine aisle at your local drugstore. Check out your favorite websites. Flip on your television. It doesn't take much effort to figure out what the current pop culture trends are. But who decides what the public "should" wear, watch, listen to, or read? The media plays a big role in setting the trends. And violence has long been a part of those trends.

Experience shows that violent books, movies, music, and sports draw a large audience. They also generate more profit for companies that rely on violence. Those companies keep creating violent entertainment and merchandise despite the effect that it might have on society. If you've experienced violence in your life, you might be forced to relive it through popular culture.

The popularity of combat sports, such as boxing, shows that there continues to be a market for violence.

Violence translates into any language, making it a popular device for filmmakers throughout the world.

Those who fear that children will become desensitized toward violence can become frustrated by the decisions of the entertainment industry.

[21ST CENTURY SKILLS LIBRARY]

Violence as entertainment is not a new concept. In ancient Rome, gladiators fought each other to entertain crowds. Today, violence remains popular with the media for a variety of reasons. One is its simplicity. It translates easily into other languages—an explosion in Japan looks like an explosion in California. It can be understood by most audiences.

But selective editing can lead to a twisted view of violence. Producers, writers, and editors don't always tell

LOVE IS RESPECT

Love is Respect is a website dedicated to awareness of domestic violence, especially among teens. Break the Cycle and the National Domestic Violence Hotline joined forces to create Love is Respect. Other media outlets such as the *New York Times, Seventeen,* The Associated Press, *Cosmopolitan,* the Huffington Post, and Perez Hilton offered their support. Love is Respect aims to educate teens and media outlets about the effects of violence displayed in the media. A tip sheet on the Break the Cycle website guides media professionals who are looking for ways to cover dating violence responsibly.

Gladiators fought for the crowd's entertainment and their own glory in ancient Rome.

the whole story. They might leave out facts that do not contain enough blood and gore or contradict the message that they want to send. And they certainly don't want to turn you away from their product. Think about the video games you play. When you kill a character, do you attend the character's funeral? Do you comfort his widow, or contribute to a scholarship fund for her children? Of course not. Those can be the consequences of violence in real life. But creators want to keep you coming back, so they will omit certain details.

GLADIATORS OF ANCIENT ROME

The citizens of ancient Rome did not have media to entertain them. Instead, they gathered in huge arenas throughout the Roman Empire. There, they watched human beings battle each other to the death. Gladiators were highly trained fighters. The History Channel described their battles as "equal parts sport, theater and cold-blooded murder."

Most gladiators were part of the lower class. Many of them were slaves and criminals. But they were seen as heroic warriors to the rest of the lower-class population. That gave the gladiators celebrity status. Children played with clay figurines of their favorite gladiators. They were the original action figures! Pottery displayed paintings of famous fights.

Much like athletes today, gladiators endorsed various products to cash in on their fame. Some were encouraged to wear certain scents on their bodies and clothes. Those scents were then sold to the public so other Romans could buy them in order to "feel like a gladiator."

WHAT THE PEOPLE WANT?

Many of the most-watched television shows in the United States contain violent content. In the 2013–14 season, the action drama *NCIS* was the second-highest rated series on TV. The gory zombie show *The Walking Dead* came in fourth. More than 18 million viewers of all ages tuned in to *The Walking Dead* each week. Those numbers tell TV networks that a lot of people enjoy watching that type of show.

But that does not mean that all media outlets push violence on their audiences. Some have fought back